Whispers of Light

Whispers of Light

JOY MEAD

wild goose
publications  www.**ionabooks**.com

First published 2019 by
Wild Goose Publications
21 Carlton Court, Glasgow G5 9JP, UK
the publishing division of the Iona Community.
Scottish Charity No. SC003794. Limited Company Reg. No. SC096243.

ISBN 978-1-84952-672-2

Cover artwork © Steve Raw | www.stephenraw.com

Overseas distribution
Australia: Willow Connection Pty Ltd, Unit 4A, 3–9 Kenneth Road,
Manly Vale, NSW 2093
New Zealand: Pleroma, Higginson Street, Otane 4170, Central Hawkes Bay
Canada: Bayard Distribution, 10 Lower Spadina Ave., Suite 400, Toronto,
Ontario M5V 2Z

Printed by Bell & Bain, Thornliebank, Glasgow

Contents

Foreword by Ron Ferguson   7
Introduction   9

Shining   12
15th January 2017   13
The in and out song of the sea   14
Stones   17
An extraordinary conversation with an ordinary stone   18
Awakening   20
A child's questions   22
Soap   23
The art of lettering   24
Let your life speak   26
There was once …   28
Cuckoo   30
Letting go   32
Life drawing   34
Emily and the labyrinth   35
Mum and Dad   38
For the love of trees …   39
Heartbreak   41
For the love …   42
Cloth   43
Whispers of light   44
Iona again   45
Seeking 46
Roots 46
Loss   47

Last leaves   48
Two winter haiku   49
At eighty   50
Candlemas flowers   52
The extraordinary quality of light   53
Pears in red wine   54
Living the moment   64
Eve in the garden   65
Self-harm   67
Translation   68
Being Mother   69
At Scarista   70
Window ledge stones   72
River   74
Meditation on reason and beauty   76
Faith   78
Creating a woodland garden   79
Walk with me   80
A way to live   81
Gift   82
Into winter   83
In my own words   85
A rare generosity   86
Thoughts from Room 7   89
At Christmas   90
I believe   91
Her voice   93

Acknowledgements and thanks   96

Foreword

I have admired, and greatly enjoyed, Joy Mead's work for some years now. She is a poet of great sensitivity, a deeply religious poet, without being a Religious Poet. Her spirituality is grounded in the depths of 'ordinary' life – the extraordinary life. Joy is one of an exceptional group of gifted poets who have emerged from the ranks of the Iona Community in comparatively recent times.

A new book by Joy is an event to treasure. Her previous work tells you that it will be good, and this latest collection, published by the excellent Wild Goose Publications, does not disappoint. Joy never rests on her well-earned laurels; her restless mind and her commitment to excellence keep her searching for new ways to touch the hearts of all. This wordsmith offers up lines that you want to roll around in your mouth before releasing them to the world. Her poem 'Skeleton of a Poem' from her collection *Glimpsed in Passing* reads thus:

Bare trees
against a darkening sky,
brachial.

Driftwood, death white
discarded bones
from unknown shores.

These beautiful, spare words cry out to be spoken aloud, savoured in the mouth. Try them. And these words from her poem 'Seeking' in this new collection, *Whispers of Light*:

Rhyme the colours.
Play with the light.
The perfect poem
Waits to be written.

So: admire, enjoy and be inspired.

Ron Ferguson

Introduction

Whispers of Light is a book of moments, illuminated moments, those times when joy breaks through, when beauty amazes and goes some way towards healing. It's also about the onus on us to enjoy. I've tried to explore relationships, memories and the living world in the light that makes a moment special, enhances its significance.

Thinking, awareness, consciousness breaks into the silence that is poetry. Perhaps I'm writing on the edge of silence, living each moment fully, moving towards the one thing that glistens out of sight … the perfect poem.

Each poem celebrates what it is to be alive and, in some way, what it is to contemplate death.

I hope each poem is:

Whispering of freedom.
Whispering that all that lives
is known and never dies
completely.

And I hope too that you might be inspired to see your own moments in a refreshed light and be amazed.

Joy Mead

ONE STONE
IN my hand.
ALL THE EARTH
at my hEart.

Shining

There is light in books:
a glow
to grace a room,
to hold the light
as any candle
might.

There is beauty,
empathy, understanding.
With words carefully handled,
white space subtly managed,
imagination shines out
in theory's dark place.

Poetry relishes the day.

15th January 2017

Thinking of you on your birthday
in the year you will marry
compels a certain humility.
What we began a wonder ago
is wholly itself now with its own
powers and passions,
choices and chances
undisturbed, yet held maybe,
by my fears or dreams.

The in and out song of the sea*

We have come down to the shore today
following the light to the dancing waves

We have come by air, by land
and by sea. We have come
with our sorrows and our joys
with our disappointments and our dreams.
We have come wishing and wondering
to play our part in a day
that holds wonder enough.

We have followed the scent of salt on the edging wind,
to a place where air and space and water are generous,
where the horizons are far and time is always early;
a harbour; for us today a touching place,
a breathing space and a threshold,
an ordinary place
we, and the sea's litany,
will make extraordinary.

We have come down to the shore today
following the light to the dancing waves

We have come with our own stories
and we have come to create
a new story for tomorrow's telling:
your story, Andrew and Leonie.

You bring the music of memory,
the past to hold and let go,
the willingness to trust the future
and each other. Today
a sea-washed stone – a silent image –
will become a sign and a promise
holding for you words to savour:
love, joy, compassion, continuity
and faithfulness.
You will create beauty in this moment
giving us all the hope
to fall in love with life again.

We have come down to the shore today
following the light to the dancing waves

Trust the tangled path
that has led you here.
Trust the blessing of wind
and water. Trust the boat,
a thing so small
on which much depends.

We wish you the safety
of the boat, the two of you,
riding the waves,
sheltered from the storm.
We wish you the sensation

of the lift of the boat:
a new exultation, fine as spindrift.
The sea with its in and out dreams
will catch you up
and carry you
into the future.

We have come down to the shore today
following the light to the dancing waves

And so, my son and my new daughter,
make the story, hold the wonder.
Let your life together speak the best
of what it means to be alive
on this earth, what it is to be human.

You sail into uncertainty
carrying within you
the beauty of this day,
safe in the light
of the unknowable heart of life
and the greatest miracle of all:
that we can love
and go on loving.

We have come down to the shore today
to be blessed by the light of the dancing waves

* I wrote this poem for Andrew (my son) and Leonie's wedding ceremony
and celebrations on the shore at Oban.

Stones

Wind and sea
shape their silence.
Waves roll them in
to the shore.
They hold the light somewhere
deeper than history.

Stones collect people.
They hoard secrets.
Stories of stones
are always
open-ended.

When I'm gone
this one in my hand
will go on collecting,
gathering, understanding,
touching and making
silent memories.

One stone
in my hand.
All the earth
at my heart.

An extraordinary conversation
with an ordinary stone

A stone from the shore*
shaped by wind and sea,
irregular, on the edge of things,
a piece of the earth
that is form
and holds light
so fine
it creates a song
in my heart;

a stone to carry my imagination
to distant mountains,
to the seashore's rhythm,
to one September day
of exceptional beauty;
a stone holding promises
made and given;

a collected treasure:
going to a place
and coming back with a stone:

there is comfort in knowing
the light on it, the light in it,
a rich source of metaphor
image and story.

How natural to take home a stone
to hold and long to know, to sense
the ongoing story
that is without ending:
a silent wish
for continuity;
a sense of life
that is in every touch.

If we keep silent
stones that shout aloud
will also sing
for joy.

* A sea-washed pebble: one was given to each
guest at my son's wedding on the seashore.

Awakening

Tones of a winter weekend
Charney Manor, February 2017

Aconites yellow the earth
with hints of beginning.

A Child in many-coloured boots
goes on a bear hunt,
searches for paw prints
among dead leaves:

a hint of story.

A lone blackbird
in the bare hedge
is disturbed into singing
its presence.

A louder wing sound
rises out of the dark ditch
as pigeons address the air.

Moon in a moment of blue
shows pink
before disappearing
into grey.

Voices speak poetry
in corners, on stairs,
and in courtyards
amid snow flurries.

Words are collected, held
like pebbles found on a beach,
put in pockets,
for tomorrow's poems.

Laughter bursts out of nowhere
and the wild geese cry across
a grey sky.

Tell your dreams
in the winter dawn.

A child's questions

If they bomb my bedroom
where will I sleep?

If they take away Daddy's benefits
how will we buy food?

If they steal our land
how will Mummy grow food
to feed the family?

If they pollute our water
what will my family drink?

If our earth is plundered
will money matter?

Soap
(For Alison)

Today you brought soap from Ghana,
a cleansing gift, bringing wholeness,
a sort of redemption.

I could feel unnamed hurts
in the lather on my hands
and know if I could weep
the tears would flow,
enough to flood out dreams.
Yet with the cleansing soap
comes the wonder of stories,
poetry, dance, to hold us,
to wonder that this is life.
Greed, fear and hate
cannot tear it apart
or quieten the beat
of every heart.
In the truth of imagination
a simple piece of soap
might begin a process
of healing and cleansing.
Life is like this.
It is what we see
and it is miracle enough.

The art of lettering*
(For Steve)

We all love to watch someone draw:
that intensity of looking
of both artist
and watcher
defines something
of our understanding of life.

To read your painted work
is to watch in imagination
the way letters are shaped
to come alive,
the way texture,
colour and form
sound the words
on paper or stone,
give expression beyond
what we think we know;
make words soar
as you attach them to a vision
and fly them like a kite.

The treasure of the words
is that they might transform.

So this work shapes the spirit
of poetry, makes
for watcher or reader
a precious mind moment
held in memory's light:
the gift of seeing
and saying as one.

* A celebration of the work of Stephen Raw
(see www.StephenRaw.com)

Let your life speak

If I have achieved anything, I hope
it is seen in other people, not me.
Bob Holman

By a winding route
we might move
towards an end, sensing
beauty in diversion, digression,
recognising senseless, off course
acts that heal; always
feeling our dependence
one upon another: fragile connection
beyond measure or name,
in our own hands only,
hope and without end.

There is the paring down to essentials:
the body thinning and weakening.
Poetry is shrinking
almost to its bones,
like trees in winter.

And one day to not be here.
Then all is memory, recalling,
bringing to mind
out of our depths.

Absence needs a new prompt,
a new order of things:

a way to think, to picture,
to share, to laugh again,
to let that one life so loved
speak through your life,
through many lives.

And to remember: as the beauty
of frost on seed heads –
the poetry will endure.

There was once …

1.
… a dark bookshop
and somewhere in that space
in the depths
of my memory, a girl
I no longer recognise,
perhaps never knew.

She stands book in hand
by the bookcase
reading, always reading.
This time Wordsworth's poems:
a small edition
with faded binding
lettered in gold. The poetry
waiting to be discovered
by that unlikely girl
who in a devotion of naming
I know is me.

I have the book still
and try to recapture
a whole life of poetry
and the discovery of poetry.
It's impossible.
The only movement is on,

slower, with quieter delights
in shadow and sunlight.
There is poetry in knowing
I was there in that bookshop
and that it mattered then
and matters now.
Where I have been
is not inconsequential
because of the power
of imagination,
because of the grace
of memory.

2.
I saw a tree once
growing out of cottage ruins
in a place of great beauty
and I left behind me there
a touch, a ghost maybe
to mingle with the memoried air.

But I took that image
of cottage and tree
on with me.

Everything it seems reverts
to woodland if left alone
for always.

Cuckoo

We wait
through the last days
of April, wait
into the middle
of May;

wait
for the familiar
two notes
to welcome spring;

wait
to record
the holy moment
of first hearing;

wait
with uneasy thoughts
of journeys, arrivals
and safe shores.

And conscious
now of our loss
we begin to grieve
absence
of something
seldom seen
feel the air heavy
with the lack
of a sound

and fear
for the future.

Letting go

A meditation on ageing

Let action go.
Make silence visible.
Savour the being time,
the beauty of emptiness.

Consider:
the waving white silence
of cow parsley that neither
reaps nor sows,

or how we might look
at the horizon on a clear day
without the need to know
what the end looks like.

Let go the longing to explain.
Ours now is only to wonder.

The mind cannot carry away within it
all that beauty has to give
yet it has room enough
for small treasures.

What is it we see
or imagine to be real and true?

I remember a sea of blue
that was, I think,
what music might mean
and I remember stealing the blue,
singing on the way home
with my arms full
of bluebells,
thinking the abundance for always
until the flowers faded
in the vase

and I began to learn
the wisdom that left the flowers
and held the looking,

the knowing that I will pass
and beauty continue
to amaze without me.

Life drawing

Will I learn,
with an artist's pencil
in my hand
how to imagine a soul,

how to show essence
in line and curve,
shape and form,

to re-create on a flat page
the being that is you.

This looking
one at another,
one soul
to another,
my essence
to your essence,
has an intense beauty.

I touch paper with pencil
and see for a brief moment
what it is to be human.

Emily and the labyrinth

Does she sense the peace,
understand where the good
way goes;
where there is rest
for the soul;
where a restless mind
is still.

Emily walks the labyrinth
with a no-purpose wisdom:
quiet, wordless, instinctive.
She steps out sure-footed
with a two year old's determination
looking at the way, following Grandma.

To her, living the moment,
it seems to matter not at all
where she is going.
And yet …
she senses
a destination
she can't name,
a sure ending beyond
her reach of knowledge.

Years later, looking
at the photograph,
it's not only Emily
who comes to mind.
I remember my dear friend Sue
who lay dying before her time,
peacefully nearing an end
that was not destination
but a reaching for the centre,
how she turns to me, waiting
by her bed:

'We know where we're going
don't we Joy?'

not wanting reassurance
but seeking solidarity
that we carry the stars,
the dreams, with us.

My 'Yes' was quiet, unsure
and troubled me.

But now I can see
the knowing
as uncertainty,
as stepping out
towards the unknowing:

not a journey   but ...
a way to be
where there is no being;
to sing
where there is no song;
the inexpressible, pure joy
of the trusting heart
and feet.

Something a tiny girl
could touch upon walking
the first steps towards ...

Mum and Dad

Sometimes I think
what I didn't do after you.
There was the opportunity not taken
of a view in the undertaker's chapel of rest
with its plastic flowers and fake grief.
And again the resisted moment
in the crematorium chapel
when the coffin moves
into soap-opera land.

Might these reflect
what I didn't do for you,
with you, when you were alive.

For the love of trees …

Once there was a spirit
in the woods, now
there's the lonely sound
of wind and rain.

All winter bare branches
move as air moves
making a mystery
of shape and form.

We talk no longer of heart
when we tell of trees.

And what then
of the movement
of our human hearts
in arteries small and smaller,
in form of trunk and branches,
in tree-like patterning.
They give life
to the muscle wall, unseen,
unless an artist imagines
or a photographer records
for medical reasons
or maybe for beauty's sake.

And as a fallen tree
might regenerate
so our struggling hearts,
our damaged hearts,
our broken hearts,
are not always beyond
repair. We know life.

In 2002 the British Heart Foundation supported
an exhibition, Tree of Life, challenging viewers
to reflect on the beauty of their inner selves
through the heart and its blood supply.

Because

Because it reminds me of butterflies
I love the smell of the forgotten nettles
when the spring sun warms them.
Because they remind me of butterflies
the nettles I never got around to clearing
take me back to summers long gone
and forward to joys yet to emerge.
Because they will bless me with butterflies
I love the life force of rampant nettles.

Heartbreak

The whisper that is rising to *the*
shout, murmur they call it, a *mewling*
protesting, stop the flow *sound*

pushing for onward rush *of*
pure blood, hinting at murmuration, *a*
pulling together, staying or *leaking*,
whole body thing – all or nothing of the *heart*.

For the love …

I could indulge the sexuality fully *but*
only by relishing the safety of carrots, *not*
allowing lush fruit, not admitting the *flail*
and ongoing, unforgiving acts of *flagellation.*

When writing the poems on this page and page 41 I
was influenced by Robin Robertson's work in his book
Swithering (Picador Poetry, 2006). 'Heartbreak' reflects
a line from his poem 'A Seagull Murmur' (see line-end
words in italics) and 'For the love' reflects a line from
'Still Life with Cardoon and Carrots' (again line-end
words in italics).

Cloth
(for Alison)

The cloth you brought from Ghana:
lagoon blue, red as blood
and tie-dyed with love.
I lay it at our feet
full of dreams
yours and mine
and others' never known.

We'll touch with care
the dreams of unknown friends.
We'll wish for them
the cloths of heaven*
from the colours of earth

and walk gently
with their dreams
spread beneath our feet
and held in our hearts.

*See 'He Wishes for the Cloths of Heaven', W.B.Yeats
from *The Wind Among the Reeds,* pub 1899.

Whispers of light

What colour are winter whispers
when the earth is cold
and the trees are bare?

Willow green-grey maybe
or they could be gold,
so quiet, rich, direct
and full of promise,

like a butterfly
at a cold winter window:
fragile, quiet thing
out of its time.
It will surely die.
Yet that I see it
and know it has lived
matters;

like the small posy on a coffin
or the dream of a voice
in a January night

whispering of freedom,
whispering that all that lives
is known and never dies
completely.

In his book *I Saw Ramallah*, Palestinian writer Mourid Barghouti says that oppressed people need direct poetry; only the free feel poetry that whispers. I had this in mind when writing the poem 'Whispers of light' …

Iona again

A returning: time on an island,
where comfort is in knowing boundaries
and small attempts to understand
what exile might mean,
to know where I am now.

Days of tangible poetry,
thoughts of the things,
of other exiles: soap and tie-dyed cloth,
or anything as diverse and odd
as cellophane jam pot covers
and brandy snaps.
This accumulation of my own
and others' memories
makes a day of deep simplicity:
a time to change, to grow,
to know homecoming.

Seeking

Rhyme the colours.
Play with the light.
The perfect poem
waits to be written.
The words out there
somewhere in the light
ask to be drawn in,
wrapped around, arranged,
to make a defence
against the dark:
a fully formed poem:
a story to live by.

Roots

As the rowan tree
roots in the rock
and withstands wind
so the holy island:
the sharp air, clear skies,
deep sense of place

is like a seed in my being
grounded in me

and knowing I must leave
I'm longing for this place
even as I'm still here.

Loss

1
How young is love
and old its tender touch
giving warmth in talk
to unlikely subjects.

How I might long
to return.

2
In the soft light this evening
I sense the approaching winter.
The nights will be different now
with cold and candles
to be snuffed out
carefully.

Last leaves

The wind is taking
the last of the leaves,
scattering gold
beneath our feet.

Thinning light comes askance
and catches by surprise
branches and a few seedpods.
The revealed beauty
of the barest trees
suggests absence
yet holds our eyes.

People don't stay out so long.
Rain seems to drown
the memory of sunshine
but a smile is left behind
when they go indoors.

Earth gives off its autumn
scent: the air is quiet.
Shadows move round
as the sun follows its course
and everything settles
to a sense of ripeness
and ending.

Two winter haiku

Cold hangs in the low light:
diamond drops
on a spider's web.

Sun breaks through
slow to touch the last leaves
with a farewell kiss.

At eighty
(for Ian)

1
There may be rumours
of approaching death,

warning buoys, masts and bells.

But today there is the sweet wood
of a boat, well-preserved,
restored and remembered,
ready to push out
into the known
and the unknown.

There is sunlight to warm
eighty year old bones,
sweet like the old timbers
and memories waiting
to be made

on this magical day:
a Hebridean blue sea;
scent and sound,
wash and wind
to carry forever
far beyond
the rumours.

2
A gift of boots
for walking
the good earth,
trekking or sauntering
towards the light
or the dark;

to release
the scent of the soil,
or feel of rocks underfoot
and the call of distant hills
where the pull up will be hard.

Let the footprints
on the earth
be light.

Let soil and blessings
sunlight and surprise
be the joy
of the day.

On sea or land,
let the blessings be
ordinary moments
lived fully,
days not seized
but cherished.

Candlemas flowers

An uneasy coming:
when you've been so long
in the winter place
you hardly expect to survive,
only to be noticed.

A hard searching
for the place beyond
desolation, to be birth flower,
winter bloom, bringing
with you understanding
of the darkness
where growing starts,
where spring has been waiting.

The first almost colour
of the year,
in the cold light,
in the raw wind,
you surprise:
your beauty like the touch
of angels wiping away tears.

You are whispering
in the wilderness:
be ready, be aware.

You are whispering
the coming
of the daffodil chorus
and the possibility
of joy.

The extraordinary quality of light

See the holly leaves bright
with winter shine, enough
to make a page shimmer,

or the twofold light
that gives a rainbow
edge to leafless branches
and so illuminates
my words,

enlightens an attempt to hold
the last white sound
of the wind, when words
are swept along, like leaves
at the edge of autumn,
into the poem,

then ask about the light within
that shines in the mind.

Pears in red wine
(for Jan)

I wonder about the pears
doubtful about so much red wine
and my memory of a recipe
passed on to me by poets.

When I open the bottle
and pour out the wine
the colour amazes me
with something of the joy
of a wedding in Cana.
It is all the summers
I have ever known.

The pears stand upright
in the pan, unconcerned
about their total immersion
in this surprising liquid.
There is something earthing
about the shape of a pear.

An hour or so of cooking
and they looked as if carved
from the wood of an ancient tree.
Their scent fills the house
with warmth and welcome.

Days later, and you've gone.
I'm still wondering.
Such evocative pears,
eaten with joy
and a hint of sadness
at the turn of the year
in snowy weather:
were they right
for a parting blessing?
Then you send a poem
to show them ordinary
yet memorable in the sharing:
'soul food in the dead of winter'
and I am the one blessed.

Winter honeysuckle
(for Anne)

On a day of small things
you brought a gift:
winter flowers,
outwitting frost,
quietly smelling
of another time.

More than …
A thought journey with cancer
September 2012 – May 2013

Where am I?
What place is this?

Fragility, vulnerability and …
mutability, that's the word,
chanciness, change,
fickleness of cells … of life.
And yet … there is still constancy
in friendship, trust, wholeness
and beauty.
There is healing and hope,
always more than …

This might be prayer
as so much more than
a mumbling of words,
as faith in the human,
in you, you and you.

Interludes with friends:
a source of wonder and hope.

Prayer is good cells.

In this different place
every edge is question
and doubt.
Uncertainty is a way of life.

❋

One house for the living
and the dead – a resurrection thought
and words might be broken threads,
like the way the spider's web
blows in the wind
and seems tethered
to nothing.

Mutability
nothing
but time.

❋

Amazing intensity of light, colour and sound.
Each leaf seems to glow. Is that the word?
No, more about being bathed in a special light,
more about the way I'm seeing.

Seeing harebells and scabious on the hill
touched memories
of that special Orkney light
that is always more than …

Leaves hang still.
The bird, the wind,
the star, the stone.
The light is all.

A friend talks of mindfulness.
Do I understand?
I feel the softness of the wind,
the scent of air, blessing.

Falling leaves, gold …
ripeness.

I saw a child with a candle today.
Where did she get such dignity,
such depth of unknowing?

Shall I too light a candle ?
Donald said he'd light one for me.
Said he'd light it at both ends.
Then he thought he'd light a bonfire,
as more appropriate he said.
I'm still pondering!

Thoughts of days,
colours of confusion,
of times and dates
and the hazy future –
joy in becoming,
a blessed uncertainty.

Love that lights all things.

Gifts: Lavender and a lavender bag …
a small child's face
and the scent of age.
Big hugs from small bodies.

❋

There are questions.
I have no one to ask but myself –
my body and my faith in my body.

❋

About a Boat – a book
Jan and I wrote –
not knowing
I'd be in this place now
and this be what it means
to contemplate
resting the oars
on my knees.

There is strength.
Listening to my heart beat.
That's prayer.

Haiku moments:

Morning mist, rain
light gathered in diamond drops
on a spider's web,

Sun is breaking through
slowly touching the last leaves
with a farewell kiss.

Elemental – the nature of haiku
stone, wind, rain, sun, light
and dark …
between islands of thought.
A tree grows out
of a cottage without a roof.
Is this a prayer?

Grass, grass, grass,
smell in the air ...

Can you smell the cut grass,
hear the leaves fall,
know the dying of the year,
in the cutting
of the lifeline?

There is much to be written.

The quiet things we do around the home.
This is what matters: the love
in dailiness, making
each small act more than itself,
opening mind and spirit.

Isn't this poetry?
Isn't this what I've been saying
for most of my life?

If this is the end
will the wonder and the hugeness
of the ordinary be remembered.

More time to think ...
or perhaps time running out
makes thinking more intense.

Conversations about seeing into the heart
of things glimpsed in passing –
that's maybe the new book?

Transcendence with
or without God.
Being content
with the holy emptiness
and no urge to fill it
with unhelpful images.

A long pause …

… to now – 70 today,
beginning or ending or neither?
Being, always being.
Too tired to know:
Is it about celebration or what?

Then suddenly it's May

Green.
Beginnings.
Poetry, always poetry …
… and beauty
and dreams of tomorrow.
As if spring has been waiting for me …

Vulnerability

Birthing and beginning,
nurturing and nourishing,
planting and digging,
gathering and harvest.

We are part of the circle
of the earth and each other.

Waking, wondering and wandering,
writing poems, telling stories,
shaping, painting and weaving,
exploring language and colour,
music and sound.

We are part of the circle
of the earth and each other

Making and living love,
changing nappies, washing floors,
baking bread, cooking meals,
touching, smelling, hearing, sharing,
celebrating and sorrowing.

We are part of the circle
of the earth and each other

Through hurting and healing,
breaking and renewal,
accepting and letting go,
dying and ending.

We are part of the circle
Of the earth and each other.

A version of this poem appears as part of 'Underneath are the Everlasting Arms' in *A Way of Knowing*, Joy Mead, Wild Goose Publications, 2012.

Living the moment

Now
no longer sure
of the past
with its memories
sorrow and joys
but ready
to redeem it
with words
yet to be born.

Now
as the wind
sings on the shore,
around the corners
of buildings
or high in the trees,
hearing the music
of being,
attending
to the one thing
as yet undiscovered,
and beyond
my perception
of happiness.

Eve in the garden

fully alive to every lovely thing:
flowers to please and delightful food
to gather and share and eat;

ordinary sounds of the day
to trust: wind in the trees,
pebbles on the tide,
the fall of a leaf,
the changing spring birdsong.

Earth is listening.
Earth is speaking.
The earth's song connects
like a well-loved hymn
or an unremembered lament
coming from a place beyond
her consciousness,
suggesting relationship,
seeking understanding,
making history
to comfort and disturb.

The earth, perhaps, returns
her love on its own terms.
Knowing begins with touch
and taste, begins
with a willingness
to see what blossoms and grows,
to feel the ache of being alive.
So amid devastation and destruction
she challenges the primacy of reason,
sees something to attend to
beyond injustice,
remakes, tells anew
the old, old story
and risks delight.

Self-harm

The glass jewel
in her navel
and rings in her ears:
all for us
to admire.

And I wonder
how these invasive trinkets
add anything
to her young beauty.

But I must smile,
and show no unease
or premonition
of where
this could lead.

Translation

Whatever else there may be
of sorrow and anger
there will be beauty
as a flower opens
or a drop of rain
rests on a leaf,
in the face
of a laughing child
or the careworn face
of age.

Even as the words are uncovered
to tell of another's anguish,
of abuse, hatred and fear
there will be beauty
as there might be
a caring hand.

The words that touch
another's anguish
also celebrate the light
of the life within her,
rejoice with her
at what might be,
make beauty the measure.

For if the only measure is injustice
where is the praise, the delight
the undying joy
of resurrection.

Being Mother

The path is winding
and most of the flowers
accidental or random,
unexpected and unplanned
yet essential.
Nettles grow in the house
of struggling dreams and a tree
reaches to the sky like a prayer.
There are whispers –
of others who stood
where we stand.

Does light come
from learning the way,
following the pattern.
Like Penelope we weave
and unweave.
We all try. We all improvise.

We fall or fly, hold or let go.
There is no single pattern
ongoing, and never will be;
only the everlasting arms
challenged, weakened,
but always open.

At Scarista

Peace seems embodied here.
Its presence is unending
as the movement of the sea
on the resisting shore.

Peace is in the fragrance
of rain on the grass,
in the wind
on the stones.

Why then in this unrestrained quiet
unease, longings not my own.
but part history, part memory
like waves of something
disturbed by a question:

Who will know what
in the emptiness, agony, oblivion
I have strived for, searched for,
hoped for and sometimes
thought I heard, or saw or felt
when new life screamed
from the silence
of every bud of May?

Who will know the fragile hope
that is only, and can only ever be,
in our human hands?

Prayer you know
doesn't become nothing
because we leave God out of it.

Earth will remember.
Death will be relevant.
All thought will be still
and the peace
of the unending sea,
of the mother earth,
will become my peace.

Window ledge stones

With a wordless sense
of their own being:
they hold hills,
ridges, slopes
and sudden drops
where water flows
where light shines.

There is continuity
in stones moulded
by a restless ocean;
tossed back and forth
with the tide,
shaped by the rhythm
and rhyme of history,
the in and out flow
of life.

Collected they're treasure
threaded, precious like jewels,
worked for beauty
or shaped for toil.

Beauty in adornment.
Beauty in use.
Symbols of renown, identity
and humanity.
Think how it shines:
that blade in its glass case.
Or how the necklace
from Skara Brae
stirs something deep
within us.

We sense a magic,
a shaping hand
and mind,
unknown, unnamed,
that listens and tells
in a collection on a shelf
of potential, relationship
and all that has ever been:

an open-ended story.

River

I grow old and it might be
as if I stand each day
alone on a river bank
alone beside a flow
I cannot see, but imagine
as it catches the light
inside me – unseen people,
unknown people moving
through space, through time.
Our nature is to flow,
to flee to safety.
I might consider
how to move forward
if there were place
to which to move,
to reach a dream,
follow a desire stronger
than any natural force.

Where are the channels for dreams,
the channels for hopes?
Beware the dams!
They restrict the flow.

The banks will burst
and create a flood
to engulf us all.
Let the river flow and form,
guiding us back to our senses
and maybe beyond;
let people find new life, bring new life
like precious water from the mountains.

We are all droplets in the same stream:
the borders or banks
that divide us from ourselves
are in our hearts and minds alone.
We are all in the flow,
all migrants through time.

Meditation on reason and beauty

I watch an orange-tip
as it settles on a periwinkle
and hold the moment
remembering alongside it
the dragonfly that once rested
on my shoulder,
the crystal drops of rainwater
on the lady's mantle leaves,
the delicate opening
of lime-green beech leaves,
the promise
of a blossoming orchard
and the hum
of insects,
the smell of the damp woods
or watercress,
a deer or a fox
as it pauses and stares
making for a moment
eye contact, strangely uplifting.

And I question:
can reason explain
the joy of these moments,
the intensity of feeling,

as my body responds
and my heart leaps
as it might also
to a painting, a poem
or piece of music,
the way I'm moved
by colour, sound, form
or the deep feeling that comes
from watching the sea,
the waves bursting on the shore,
the sense of something timeless?

These patterns of being
and being alive
delight without dominating.

We might search
for purpose or meaning
but do we understand
the commitment to enjoy,
do we understand
the noble sense, the desire
for what is right and good,
aroused by beauty.

Faith

It was the way the sun came out:
as if there was light
at the end of the tunnel,
as if there was good
to be illuminated.

The word 'Yes' –
the affirmation
that the tinsel
would never
outshine the sunlight

and something of yesterday
would be valued tomorrow.

For there will be
tomorrow
and it will be
good.

Grace,
epiphany,
spots of time,
moments of being –
as if this almost nostalgia,

this remembering, this being here,
as if there might be angels
telling us to believe in tomorrow.

Creating a woodland garden

Trees can start their lives
perfectly well
without being stuck in the ground
by humans.

An unplanned arboretum
might surprise us.
It's what happens
while we stand back
un-doing.

As for the trees,
so for dandelions,
ground elder, buttercups
Learn to love the unexpected,
sometimes unwanted,
and whole lives change.

Walk with me

Around the room
a circle of Friends
settled, relaxed,
all action stilled
but thought so active
it's almost tangible.

My eyes rest a moment
on each pair of shoes
taking in the diversity:
imagining the stories:
some have been in the soil,
collected a leaf or two –
they are happy outside;
others look soft,
easy on feet –
like the comfort of home.
Many are worn
with style and energy
anticipating the day
ahead.

I wonder about a wordless call
I hear in this room:
the journey is always long
and to walk a while

in someone else's shoes
is a silent and appropriate
gift.

A way to live

The visible silence
of cow parsley,
an exquisite white mantle;
the stone in my hand
rough and smooth, sea washed
with memories;
a picture of a woman
who toils unregarded
in distant fields
who may yet feed the world;
the returning goldfinches: treasure
unwrought by human hands;
memory of snowlight, flakes falling
 – wanting Christmas;
greylag geese – the beauty of formation.

We all need such images
in our lives.
We all need a sea washed
stone in our hands.

This might be the poetry
of everyday living; the wonder
of ordinary things; the value
of what is common and quiet.

The deep knowing
that life is real; love is good.
Everything else is held by this
and will hold us to be the beauty
that is a moment in the mind,
to be the justice and the love.

Each living thing gives its life to this
and that gift is prayer.

Gift

On a washed out winter day
imagination colours our thoughts
and makes us content to wait
for summer leaves to come again,
content to look for quiet surprises
in the rhythm and change
of earth's winter song.

Into winter

Just the tips of the trees
touched with change, edged
leaf by golden leaf
not falling yet, but waiting.
We know we must walk
on fallen leaves into winter.
The last dream of the year fades
in a burst of gold
and is gone.

So for us minutes hasten on.
Time passes grey hair by grey hair –
the wonder of life could be told in hair –
until suddenly it's winter
and I'm old,
mature, ripe maybe,
and heading home
over the fallen leaves,

loving the softness, the golden light,
and holding a lifetime of thoughts,
letting go and moving
towards essential form,
towards the naked stillness
of a bare tree, stripped

to something beyond self,
not giving way
but marking place.

Poetry, shrinking
almost to the bones,
plays out the years
like the sound of a solo flute
across a gulf from someone
to somewhere.

Do I want to re-find, amid fallen leaves
and the sound of apples falling,
who I was once
or can I accept that
there is only who I am
and that she will die?

Yet the raindrops glitter still
on the lady's mantle leaves.
After everything, at the end,
in spite of all that hurts
it's all so outrageously beautiful.

In my own words

I am woman,
groping amongst distorted symbols
for a missing life experience,
witnessing even now to a different voice,
an alternative pattern;
seeking the necessary self-knowledge
from within;
seeking the necessary definition
by my own means.

The language long sought after
is now coming to painful birth.
I see women standing in their own pain;
singing their own songs;
striving for a different measure
of human qualities;
seeking to redeem
Adam's dream.

A rare generosity

At borders, checkpoints,
gates and doorways
at the barrels of guns;

in the dark
by the sea,
a child cradled
in his arms;

in endless queues,
praying at gates,
a presence and a protest;

beside the dying
anxious and wondering;

Every day, year in, year out,
all over the world
someone, somewhere
is waiting

for the pain to end
for the joy to begin;

for healing …
and for hope.

for the first green shoots,
the first warm rays,
the cuckoo's call
and the sound of spring rain;

for the change in the tide
and the rise in the wind
to fill the sails.

Every day, year in, year out,
all over the world
someone, somewhere
is waiting

bridging the gap
between being and doing,
waiting for life and light
and a baby's cry
in the darkest times

imagining …

Thoughts from Room 7*

This garret room
has no status:
it's a tiny space,
as if for a bird,
to retreat into
and watch
under the eaves.

But the window is magical:
framing a picture of sunrise
over fields and graveyard;
or a sculpture of moss
and lichen on stone roof tiles
close enough to touch.

It's an opening
to look from,
purposefully, remembering
stories and apples,
walnuts and colours,
feet around a room,
conversation and kindness.
And to allow in … what?
The spirit, the other,
something beyond expression

or maybe, as I watch
people below
walking to and fro,
that rich sense of dependence
upon one another:
the fragile hope that is
and can only be
in our own hands.

* Room 7 is a small room – maybe once a servant's room –
on the second floor of Charney Manor, a lovely Quaker Re-
treat House in Oxfordshire where I was spending a weekend
with a local Quaker group exploring stories, poetry, colour
and friendships. I stayed at Charney Manor many times,
nearly always in this room!

At Christmas …

… so many unassuming gifts
in cards, treasured
as a little time
wisely given:
words and wonderings,
thoughts and thank-yous,
memories and moments,
to enjoy fully and gently.

Like each carefully chosen bauble
for the tree, a pleasure

and a reminder
that moments
I might enjoy
but don't
are lost for ever.

I believe

in not quite knowing:
in ambiguity, curiosity, irony
and joy

I believe in a silent understanding
that outsteps reason or sense
and allows weeping

    for untold sadness
    and lost hopes,

    for abandoned truth
    and betrayed goodness.

In a world that celebrates
instant gratification,

personal gain
and obscene wealth
it would probably be best
to find peace
in learning not to care

And yet I believe
there are unstated truths
and unimaginable hopes.

I believe that
through the tears,
and the darkness,
out of the mourning
and the lament
is the human creativity:
music, art, song, story
and the poem,
always the poem
of the golden silence
that is the not quite knowing
and the future flowering.

Her voice

Hagar outside
the circle awaits the poet
to speak for her pain.

Acknowledgements and thanks

My thanks to the various family members and friends, some identified in poem dedications, others unnamed, who have inspired many of these poems just by being who they are.

I'm deeply grateful to Ron Ferguson for contributing a Foreword; to Stephen Raw for another beautiful cover and to Wild Goose Publications, especially Sandra, for careful and sensitive handling of my writing. I also value the friendship, support and encouragement I receive from them all.

Joy Mead

ONE STONE
IN my hand.
ALL the EARTH
at my HEART.

Wild Goose Publications, the publishing house of the Iona Community established in the Celtic Christian tradition of Saint Columba, produces books, e-books, CDs and digital downloads on:

- holistic spirituality
- social justice
- political and peace issues
- healing
- innovative approaches to worship
- song in worship, including the work of the Wild Goose Resource Group
- material for meditation and reflection

For more information:

Wild Goose Publications
The Iona Community
21 Carlton Court, Glasgow, G5 9JP, UK

Tel. +44 (0)141 429 7281
e-mail: admin@ionabooks.com

or visit our website at
www.ionabooks.com
for details of all our products and online sales